Sports Illustrated KIDS

PRO FILES:
BASEBALL

WITHDRAWN

Intel on Today's Biggest Stars
AND
Tips on How to Play Like Them

Managing Editor, Sports Illustrated Kids **Bob Der**

Project Editor **Andrea Woo**

Creative Director **Beth Bugler**

Director of Photography **Marguerite Schropp Lucarelli**

Photo Editor **Annmarie Avila**

Writers **Albert Chen,
Gary Gramling, Joe Lemire**

Editors **Justin Tejada, Sachin Shenolikar**

Copy Editor **Megan Collins**

Reporter **Ryan Hatch**

Designer **Mary Mathieux**

Imaging **Geoffrey Michaud,
Dan Larkin, Robert Thompson**

Special thanks to: Myles Ringel, Jeffrey Kaji,
Georgia Millman-Perlah, Alex Borinstein,
Peyton Frazier, Jarret Harrison

Time
HOME ENTERTAINMENT

TIME HOME ENTERTAINMENT
Publisher **Richard Fraiman**
Vice President, Business Development & Strategy **Steven Sandonato**
Executive Director, Marketing Services **Carol Pittard**
Executive Director, Retail & Special Sales **Tom Mifsud**
Executive Director, New Product Development **Peter Harper**
Editorial Director **Stephen Koepp**
Director, Bookazine Development & Marketing **Laura Adam**
Publishing Director **Joy Butts**
Finance Director **Glenn Buonocore**
Assistant General Counsel **Helen Wan**
Assistant Director, Special Sales **Ilene Schreider**
Design & Prepress Manager **Anne-Michelle Gallero**
Book Production Manager **Susan Chodakiewicz**
Brand Manager **Allison Parker**
Associate Prepress Manager **Alex Voznesenskiy**
Special thanks: Christine Austin, Jeremy Biloon, Jim Childs, Rose Cirrincione,
Jacqueline Fitzgerald, Christine Font, Jenna Goldberg, Lauren Hall, Carrie Hertan,
Hillary Hirsch, Suzanne Janso, Amy Mangus, Robert Marasco, Kimberly Marshall,
Amy Migliaccio, Nina Mistry, Dave Rozzelle, Adriana Tierno, Vanessa Wu

ISBN 10: 1-60320-926-3
ISBN 13: 978-1-60320-926-7

We welcome your comments and suggestions about Sports Illustrated Kids Books.
Please write to us at:
Sports Illustrated Kids Books, Attention: Book Editors, P.O. Box 11016,
Des Moines, IA 50336-1016. If you would like to order any of our hardcover
Collector's Edition books, please call us at 1-800-327-6388, Monday through
Friday, 7 a.m. to 8 p.m., or Saturday, 7 a.m. to 6 p.m., Central Time.

1 QGV 11

JUSTIN VERLANDER

Detroit Tigers pitcher,
2011 American League Cy Young Award
winner and MVP

CONTEN

All stats in this book are through the 2011 season.

PRO FILE:
ALBER

TEAM: **ST. LOUIS CARDINALS**

POSITION: **FIRST BASEMAN**

HT: **6' 3"**   WT: **230 LBS.**

BIRTH DATE: **JANUARY 16, 1980**

HOMETOWN: **SANTO DOMINGO, DOMINICAN REPUBLIC**

PUJOLS

BACKGROUND REPORT

>> As one of the greatest sluggers of his generation, Albert Pujols has hit many home runs that have reached legendary — and almost mythical — status. There was the home run he hit as a senior at Liberty (Missouri) High, a drive that sailed over the 402-foot fence in centerfield and crashed into an air-conditioning unit atop a two-story building. There was the moon shot he launched as a college sophomore over the leftfield wall of Highland (Kansas) Community College, which soared across a street and over a tree. There was the game-winning three-run dinger in the ninth inning in Game 5 of the 2005 NL Championship Series that landed over the train tracks beyond leftfield at Houston's Minute Maid Park. And there was his ninth-inning blast on the night he had the greatest offensive game in World Series history, a missile to leftfield at Rangers Ballpark in Game 3 of the 2011 Fall Classic that made him only the third player in history to hit three home runs in a World Series game.

>>All-Time Great

Asking Pujols to pick the greatest and most memorable home run of his career is a little like asking Michelangelo to choose his favorite work of art. "I've been fortunate to have so many amazing moments in my career, it's hard to choose one home run that's more special than another," says Pujols. "When my career is over, maybe then I'll be able to look back, and maybe then, one will stand out."

CONTACT SPORT
A three-time NL MVP, Pujols had the highest career batting average (.329) among active players through 2011.

When that time comes, Pujols will undoubtedly be reflecting on one of the greatest careers in major league history. Few players have accomplished what Pujols has in 11 seasons: 10 All-Star selections, three National League MVP awards, and two World Series rings. "He's a player that you'll tell your grandkids you played with," says Cardinals rightfielder Lance Berkman. "It's a privilege to be able to watch him play."

>>Straight to the Top

Baseball has always been in Pujols's blood. His father, Bienvenido, was an accomplished

softball pitcher in the Dominican Republic. As a boy in Santo Domingo, little Albert would proudly wear his father's jersey around the neighborhood. He lived the typical life of a Dominican boy, playing baseball on scraggly fields in his neighborhood, using limes as balls and milk cartons as gloves.

Pujols, who moved to Missouri with his father when he was 16, was an accomplished high school player in Independence, Missouri, and at Maple Woods Community College in Kansas City. But he wasn't drafted until the 13th round of the 1999 amateur draft, when the Cardinals selected him. Pujols wasted little time in showing the teams that had passed on him that they had made a very big mistake. He jumped from A ball to Triple A in his first minor league season. The next spring, in 2001, when he was a non-roster invitee to Cardinals training camp, he played his way onto the big league roster in spring training. After one of the greatest rookie seasons in history — he hit .329 with 37 homers and 130 RBIs — Tony La Russa, then the Cardinals manager, signed a photo he had taken with Pujols and wrote, "To Albert, The best player I've ever coached."

Ten years later, La Russa's words rang very true as he and Pujols celebrated their second championship together after the Cardinals defeated the Rangers in the 2011 World Series. Now the manager was ready to heap even more praise. "Not only is he the best player I've managed, but when you talk about the great players in the history of the game, Albert's in the discussion," says La Russa. "There's no doubt he'll go down as one of the greats."

INSIDE INFORMATION

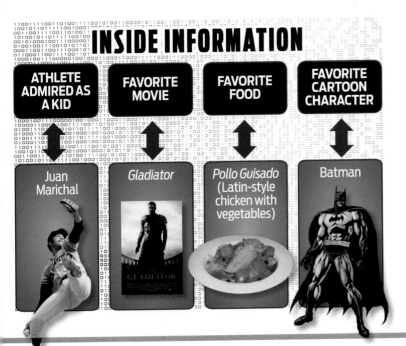

ATHLETE ADMIRED AS A KID	FAVORITE MOVIE	FAVORITE FOOD	FAVORITE CARTOON CHARACTER
Juan Marichal	Gladiator	Pollo Guisado (Latin-style chicken with vegetables)	Batman

RUNNING THE NUMBERS

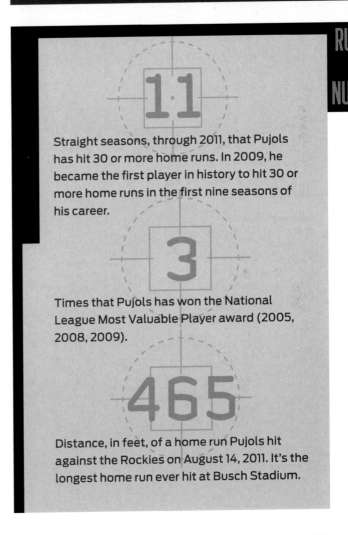

11
Straight seasons, through 2011, that Pujols has hit 30 or more home runs. In 2009, he became the first player in history to hit 30 or more home runs in the first nine seasons of his career.

3
Times that Pujols has won the National League Most Valuable Player award (2005, 2008, 2009).

465
Distance, in feet, of a home run Pujols hit against the Rockies on August 14, 2011. It's the longest home run ever hit at Busch Stadium.

SECRETS TO HIS GAME

Stand at the Plate Like Albert Pujols

Pujols holds his hands level with his right ear and bounces his right elbow three or four times to keep his hands relaxed. "If you're too stiff, then your hands can't be that quick," says Pujols.

Pujols does not take a big step with his front foot when he swings. Instead, he drives forward with his hips.

When Pujols steps up to the plate, he settles into his batting stance with his feet spread wide apart and with about 60 percent of his weight on his back foot.

POWER SURGE

Coaches say that the key to Pujols's swing is his hand speed. Because he can react faster than a lot of hitters, Pujols sees the ball for a longer period of time before he swings. And when he connects, he has the muscles to drill the ball — like he did here during Game 3 of the 2011 World Series — thanks to weightlifting that strengthens his forearms and wrists. "His hand strength is incredible," says Cardinals rightfielder Lance Berkman.

MIND GAME

You may not be able to duplicate Pujols's strength, but you can copy his approach to the game. "This game is mental more than physical," says Cardinals hitting coach Mark McGwire. "Number 5 is probably the strongest mental person I've ever been around. He's also the most prepared." Pujols studies videos of pitchers like they are math problems. After each game, he goes to a video room to review his swing to make sure that his approach remains consistent. That thorough understanding of the game allows Pujols to make the most of each plate appearance. "I can count on one hand the number of at-bats I've seen him give away," says McGwire.

IN HIS WORDS

" My strength is that I'm a smart player. If someone tells me to do something, I change it quickly. If there's something wrong with my hitting, tell me what's wrong and I'll pick it up right away. That's the best thing I have — my ability to listen to a coach and fix what I'm doing wrong.**"**

PLAYER ANALYSIS

[+] Pujols's swing is a thing of
[+] beauty. It is a simple but
[+] flawless stroke that
[+] generates staggering power.
[+] "He's able to repeat it over
[+] and over," says Berkman.
[+] Pujols covers the whole plate
[+] and often drives the ball even
[+] harder to the opposite field
[+] than he does when he's
[+] pulling the ball.
[+]   Pujols uses different bats
[+] depending on if he's facing
[+] lefthanded or righthanded
[+] pitchers. Against lefties, he
[+] swings a 33-ounce bat. When
[+] he's up against a righty,
[+] Pujols uses a bat that's one
[+] ounce lighter in order to keep
[+] him from trying to pull the
[+] ball. As a result, he rarely

[+] strikes out.
[+] "Lefthander,
[+] righthander, soft
[+] thrower, power guy,
[+] fastballs away,
[+] fastballs in — he
[+] doesn't have any
[+] holes," says McGwire.
[+]   But Pujols's
[+] greatness goes
[+] beyond what he does at the
[+] plate. After switching from
[+] outfield to first base in 2004,
[+] he evolved into one of the top
[+] fielders in the game, winning
[+] a Gold Glove in 2006 and
[+] 2010. "People overlook his
[+] defense," says former
[+] Cardinals manager Tony
[+] La Russa, "but he's the
[+] whole package."

TEAM: **TAMPA BAY RAYS**

POSITION: **THIRD BASEMAN**

HT: **6' 2"**   WT: **210 LBS.**

BIRTH DATE: **OCTOBER 7, 1985**

HOMETOWN: **DOWNEY, CALIFORNIA**

PRO FILE: EVAN NGORIA

BACKGROUND REPORT

>> When Evan Longoria arrived in Tampa to make his major league debut in April 2008, it was a little bittersweet. Longoria had reached the big leagues — but he was joining one of the worst teams in baseball. The Rays had lost 60 percent of their games, averaging 97.2 losses per season. No other franchise averaged more than 97 losses per year from 1998 through 2007. The team had never come within 18 games of an American League East division title.

But by the end of the season, all that had changed. With Longoria leading the way, Tampa *won* 97 games, topped the mighty New York Yankees and Boston Red Sox for the AL East crown, and — perhaps most surprising of all — went on to play in the World Series. After that, the Rays just kept on winning, making the playoffs in two of the next three seasons.

>>Long Road to Success

Tampa has had great players during its successful run: speedy leftfielder Carl Crawford, slugging first baseman Carlos Peña, and flame-throwing lefthander David Price among them. But Longoria has been the most valuable Ray and the team's leader. A big reason why is his constant drive to improve. "I definitely think with a lot of hard work, I can be a better player than I was [the previous] year," says Longoria. "And hopefully, [I'll] continue to raise the bar every year."

It was a long climb to the top for Longoria. Even though he was an all-conference player at St. John Bosco High School in southern California, he wasn't drafted by a major league club out of high school and didn't receive any scholarship offers to play college baseball. Instead Longoria, then a slender shortstop, played his freshman year at Rio Hondo Community College in Whittier, California.

"I'd be the first to tell you that coming out of high school, even junior college, I wasn't ready," Longoria once told reporters. "I couldn't play on this stage. I was skinnier, and as I grew physically, I grew baseball-wise."

At Rio Hondo, Longoria had an all-state season that caught the eye of Long Beach State University coaches. The following year, he transferred to LBSU, a top-notch program, for his sophomore season. The 49ers already had a star shortstop, future Colorado Rockies All-Star Troy Tulowitzki, so Longoria had to move to third base. He quickly became one of the best players in the amateur ranks, playing dazzling defense at third and hitting .336 in two seasons with LBSU. The once-unknown high school player was drafted third overall by Tampa in 2006. He hit .315 with 18 home runs in only 62 minor league games later that year, then hit .299 with 26 homers in 2007, his first full season as a professional.

Going into 2008, Longoria was considered by scouts to be among the best prospects in the AL. Rays manager Joe Maddon called him "the poster child of a new beginning."

SURE-HANDED
Longoria switched from shortstop to third base while at Long Beach State and has excelled at the position ever since.

>>Reaching Stardom

When Tampa third baseman Willy Aybar went down with an injury in early 2008, Longoria got his chance in the big leagues. He hit .272 with 27 home runs and 85 RBIs and won the Rookie of the Year award that season. But the playoffs were when Longoria really started to shine. He hit six home runs in his first 11 postseason games, leading the Rays to the World Series. Even though they lost to the Phillies in five games, it was an amazing turnaround for Tampa.

Longoria went on to be an All-Star in 2009 and '10, but missed parts of 2011 due to injury. It looked like a lost season for Longoria and Tampa until September rolled around. The Rays went on a tear, winning 16 of 24 games to catch up to Boston in the AL wild card standings heading into the last day of the season. In a must-win game, Tampa trailed 7–0 against the Yankees before Longoria's three-run home run in the eighth inning helped close the gap. Then, with one out in the bottom of the 12th, he ripped a pitch over the leftfield wall to send Tampa back to the playoffs.

"It was truly astonishing," Maddon said of the home run. "But it was believable that [Longoria] would do it."

INSIDE INFORMATION

ATHLETE ADMIRED AS A KID	FAVORITE MOVIE	FAVORITE FOOD	FAVORITE CARTOON CHARACTER
Michael Jordan	*The Sandlot*	Steak and potatoes	Superman

BASEBALL RÉSUMÉ

COLLEGE
Rio Hondo Community College (2004),
Long Beach State University (2005–06)

MINOR LEAGUE TEAMS
Hudson Valley, Visalia, Montgomery, Durham
(2006–08)

MAJOR LEAGUE TEAM
Tampa Bay Rays (2008–present)

CAREER STATS

GP	AVG	HR	RBI
563	.274	113	401

RUNNING THE NUMBERS

113
Career home runs hit by Longoria through 2011, the second-most among AL third basemen over the span of their first four years in the big leagues.

3
All-Star appearances for Longoria in his first three seasons. He is the only third baseman to be an All-Star in each of his first three years.

28
First-place votes, out of 28, that Longoria received in 2008 to become the AL Rookie of the Year. He was the first unanimous Rookie of the Year in either league since the St. Louis Cardinals' Albert Pujols in 2001.

SECRETS TO HIS GAME

Play the Infield Like Evan Longoria

Mistakes in the field are often caused by poor fundamentals. Baseball's best defensive infielders know how to put themselves into a position to get to the ball and make a good throw. Longoria's natural athleticism allows him to pull off jaw-dropping plays at the hot corner, but his fundamentally sound approach plays a big role too. Here are three tips from Longoria to help you become a better infielder.

[1]

"When the pitch is being thrown, I make sure I'm in an athletic position," Longoria says. "That's different for everyone, but you should have your knees bent and your balance centered so you're ready to move laterally either way."

[2]

When a ground ball comes your way, try to take it one step at a time. You want to first get in front of the ball before thinking about the throw. "No matter what, just make sure the ball ends up in your glove," says Longoria.

[3]

Once you have the ball, then it's time to make the throw. If your momentum is taking you away from your target, be sure to set your feet. "When you're setting up to throw, there should be a straight line from your back shoulder to your front shoulder pointing toward the base," says Longoria. "You want your momentum going toward your target."

KNOW THE DRILL

Improving your infield defense often comes down to simple repetition. When he was growing up in southern California, Longoria had to be resourceful to get his fielding practice in. "I had a brick wall in my backyard, so I would throw a baseball against it to get used to fielding grounders," he says. Longoria's mom would get in on the training too, feeding him ground balls. "She would have me moving side to side, really having to reach for them," Longoria says. "She made it tough!"

PLAYER ANALYSIS

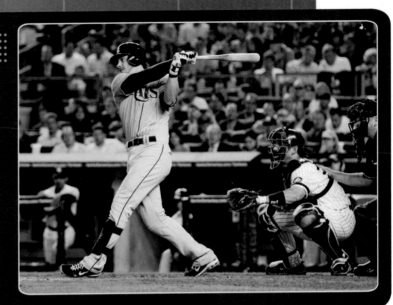

[+] Great hitters like Longoria
[+] have more than just strength.
[+] "He has tremendous balance,"
[+] says a scout from an opposing
[+] team. "He's a lot like Ryan
[+] Braun. Both of those guys hit
[+] the same way they did in
[+] college. When you [get to the
[+] pros] and don't have to make
[+] a lot of adjustments, it means
[+] you're very gifted."

[+] Longoria has the power to
[+] pull the ball over the leftfield
[+] wall, but he can also drive the
[+] ball to the opposite field. "He
[+] uses the entire field," says the
[+] scout, "and he's smart enough
[+] to know when he has a chance
[+] to take a shot at driving the
[+] ball out of the park."

[+] Longoria's natural
[+] athleticism is most obvious in
[+] the field. The two-time Gold
[+] Glove winner is arguably the
[+] best defensive third baseman
[+] in baseball, with the range to
[+] get to ground balls that would
[+] normally go through the
[+] infield for a base hit.

[+] "He's more athletic than
[+] other third basemen, without
[+] a doubt," says the scout. "He
[+] has a great first step and

[+] great anticipation, and he's
[+] always in good position. [My]
[+] grading scale for arm
[+] strength is 20 to 80, and he
[+] has a 70 arm. His throws to
[+] second base for double plays
[+] are [usually] right on
[+] the mark.

[+] "The Rays always surprise
[+] people, and he's a big part of
[+] that. He is a true star," says
[+] the scout.

IN HIS WORDS

" I take a lot of pride in my defense. People get caught up in the offensive stats, the home runs, but it's like basketball. Everyone wants to be the scorer, but the guys who play the best defense win the games."

PRO FILE:

ROY HA

TEAM: **PHILADELPHIA PHILLIES**

POSITION: **PITCHER**

HT: **6' 6"**   WT: **230 LBS.**

BIRTH DATE: **MAY 14, 1977**

HOMETOWN: **ARVADA, COLORADO**

LLADAY

BACKGROUND REPORT

>> When they were looking for a new home in the Denver area more than 30 years ago, the Halladay family had a very specific request: The house had to have a basement that was at least 60 feet long. Roy Halladay Jr., a commercial airline pilot, had big plans to build a batting cage and a pitching mound for his son, Roy III. The Halladays eventually found a house in Arvada, Colorado, with a basement large enough for young Roy to throw off a mound and fire baseballs through a tire and into a mattress.

The baseball education of the Philadelphia Phillies' Roy Halladay began in that basement, but there would be many more lessons to come.

>>Study Sessions

Two books helped make Halladay one of the best pitchers in baseball. When he was 13, he read Nolan Ryan's *Pitcher's Bible* and began following the book's training programs almost obsessively. Halladay learned all about proper pitching techniques and weight-training regimens, and by the time he was a senior at Arvada West High, he was one of the most sought-after hurlers in the country. He was a tall and skinny power pitcher with an over-the-top throwing motion that unleashed devastating fastballs.

The Toronto Blue Jays drafted Halladay out of high school in the first round of the 1995 draft, and three years later, he was in the majors, pitching like a polished

veteran. In only his second major league start, he was one out away from a no-hitter before giving up a home run. But Halladay would struggle over the next few seasons. In 2001 he was performing so poorly that when the Blue Jays demoted him all the way down to Class A, Halladay wondered if he should quit baseball altogether. "I had lost confidence in myself," he says. "From the age of 8 to 22, I'd never had a doubt. But I was facing adversity for the first time, and I had no idea how to turn it around."

While Halladay was at Toronto's spring training facility working

WORKHORSE
From 2007 through '11 Halladay led the league in complete games with 42.

with pitching instructors, his wife, Brandy, gave him a book called *The Mental ABC's of Pitching*, written by sports psychologist Harvey Dorfman. The book became Halladay's instructional manual, as he completely revamped his over-the-top delivery (he started throwing with a lower arm angle) and began restoring his confidence. Halladay returned to the Blue Jays, and two years later he won the American League Cy Young Award. He would win the NL award in 2010, as the ace of the Phillies. Even after more than 10 seasons in the majors — he's been named an All-Star eight times — he still reads *The Mental ABC's of Pitching* several times a season.

>>Attention to Detail

Halladay has four nasty pitches — a curveball, cutter, split-finger, and four-seam fastball — but what sets him apart from his peers is his work ethic. He's usually the first one at the ballpark before games and the last one to leave. "He's the most prepared guy," says Phillies manager Charlie Manuel. "He works harder than anybody I've ever seen."

How meticulous is Halladay? He catalogues every start, every bullpen session, every workout, and every batter he's ever faced in notebooks and in his computer. Says Halladay, "What gives me confidence going into a game is knowing that I had prepared the best I possibly could."

HIGH SCHOOL
Arvada West

MINOR LEAGUE TEAMS
GCL Blue Jays, Dunedin, Knoxville, Syracuse (1995–98)

MAJOR LEAGUE TEAMS
Toronto Blue Jays (1998–2009),
Philadelphia Phillies (2010–present)

CAREER STATS

GP	W	SO	ERA
378	188	1,934	3.23

RUNNING THE NUMBERS

2

No-hitters thrown by Halladay in 2010. He tossed a perfect game in May against the Marlins and threw the second no-hitter in playoff history against the Reds in October. Halladay is the only major leaguer to throw no-hitters in the regular season and postseason.

8

Seasons Halladay has thrown more than 200 innings. He led the majors in innings pitched in 2002, '03, '08, and '10.

2

Cy Young Awards given to Halladay, who won the AL award in 2003, as a member of the Blue Jays, and the NL award in 2010, with the Phillies.

INSIDE INFORMATION

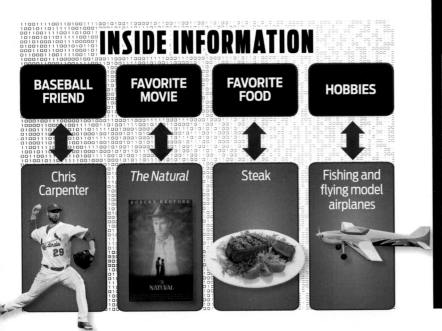

BASEBALL FRIEND	FAVORITE MOVIE	FAVORITE FOOD	HOBBIES
Chris Carpenter	*The Natural*	Steak	Fishing and flying model airplanes

SECRETS TO HIS GAME

On Repeat

Halladay is a creature of routine. "I try to be as consistent as possible and pay close attention to detail," he says. In between starts, he lifts weights, uses an elliptical machine, runs on a treadmill, and soaks in a tub, which helps his body recover faster. On days that he starts, he won't speak to anyone before games. His pregame bullpen session is always the same: He throws 35 pitches, in five-pitch sequences broken down by different types of pitches — four-seam fastballs, cutters, change-ups, curveballs. Halladay makes sure that every pitch is thrown from the same release point. During his starts, he sits in the same spot in the dugout.

PERFECT YOUR MECHANICS LIKE ROY HALLADAY

Halladay is proof that a change in mechanics can make all the difference for a pitcher. What are the keys to a proper delivery? "Balance, direction, finish, and keeping your head on line," says A's minor league pitching coordinator Gil Patterson, who coached Halladay in the Blue Jays organization. To work those skills, Patterson recommends drawing a line in the dirt, aimed toward home plate. For righthanders, stand with the ball of your back foot on the line and the toes facing third base. (For lefties, your back foot would face first base.) As you stand, "all the weight is in the back side," says Patterson. The line represents a "tunnel that you stay in, with all the weight transferring to the front foot as you throw." The front foot should land on the line, not pointed straight at the target but turned slightly in. You don't need to throw a ball or bring up your back leg like you would when you pitch. Just practice the motion so that you get used to the way it feels. Says Patterson, "Rotating your hips and keeping your head on a line are keys."

PLAYER ANALYSIS

[+] Halladay is tough to hit
[+] because of the vicious
[+] movement on his pitches.
[+] "The action on his ball is
[+] ridiculous," says Cardinals
[+] rightfielder Lance Berkman.

[+] "The ball is at your eyeballs,
[+] then before you know it, it's at
[+] your ankles." Halladay's
[+] fastball was straight until he
[+] began working on changing
[+] his delivery with Blue Jays
[+] minor league coaches,
[+] including Mel Queen and
[+] Gil Patterson. Instead of
[+] throwing the ball over the top,
[+] Halladay began throwing it
[+] from a three-quarters angle.
[+] "He started twisting his wrist
[+] a little bit, too," says
[+] Patterson, "and the way the
[+] ball started moving, it was like
[+] he was throwing a Wiffle ball."

[2]

[3]

IN HIS WORDS

"After being sent to the minors [in 2001], I told myself that if I was going to be out of baseball, I wanted to be able to look back and say I did everything to the best of my ability. I realized that I was going to have to go the extra mile from that point on. No cutting corners. The extra things are what separates people."

TEAM: MINNESOTA TWINS

POSITION: CATCHER

HT: 6' 5" **WT: 235 LBS.**

BIRTH DATE: APRIL 19, 1983

HOMETOWN: ST. PAUL, MINNESOTA

PRO FILE: JOE MAUER

BACKGROUND REPORT

>> When he was in high school, Joe Mauer was in a position that many young athletes would be jealous of. He had to make the tough decision to become either one of baseball's top prospects or college football's next great quarterback.

As a senior at Cretin-Derham Hall High School (St. Paul, Minnesota) in 2000–01, Mauer became the first athlete selected as the *USA Today* High School Player of the Year in two sports. As a quarterback, he threw for 3,022 yards and 41 touchdowns, including a state-record-tying seven TDs in the regional finals. For the baseball team, he batted .605 and hit home runs in seven consecutive games, tying a national record. He signed a letter of intent to play quarterback for Florida State, which had just won a national title. But when the hometown Minnesota Twins made him the Number 1 overall pick of the 2001 MLB draft, Mauer chose the big leagues. "[As a kid] I followed Kent Hrbek and Kirby Puckett," Mauer said of the Twins legends. "It's unbelievable to look down and see Twins [on my uniform]."

HOMETOWN HERO

A native of St. Paul, Minnesota, Mauer chose baseball over college football when he was drafted by the Twins.

>>Worth the Wait

Mauer wasn't ready for the majors right away. He spent three seasons in the minors, and during that time a lot of people felt the Twins may have made a mistake by drafting him. Mauer was a promising prospect, but the Number 2 pick in his draft, Chicago Cubs pitcher Mark Prior, had already emerged as a star.

It took a few years, but Mauer proved Minnesota right. He made his big league debut on Opening Day in 2004 as a 20-year-old, getting two hits and two walks in five trips to the plate. A knee injury cut his season short, but Mauer still hit .308 with 15 extra-base hits in 35 games. Two seasons later, he won his first batting title, hitting .347 and making his first All-Star team. In 2009, Mauer added some power to his game, slugging a career-high 28 home runs to go along with a .365 batting average. He won the American League MVP award in a landslide vote.

>>Position Change?

Mauer is more than just a force at the plate, though. Playing one of the most physically demanding positions, he also takes pride in his work *behind* the plate. "I want to take care of the defense first," Mauer has said. "That's a big part of the game."

Catching has taken a toll on Mauer in recent years. In 2011, he missed 80 games with back and knee injuries, and he hit a career-low .287 when he was in the lineup. By the end of the 2011 season the Twins had started using him at first base. So what did his teammates think of Mauer's ability to gobble up ground balls? "Pretty incredible," said Carl Pavano, the starting pitcher when Mauer made his debut at first. Mauer has already gone from star QB to top-notch catcher to batting champion. Don't be surprised if he adds Gold Glove first baseman to the list.

HIGH SCHOOL
Cretin-Derham Hall

MINOR LEAGUE TEAMS
Elizabethton, Quad Cities, Fort Myers, New Britain, Rochester (2001–04)

MAJOR LEAGUE TEAM
Minnesota Twins (2004–present)

CAREER STATS

GP	AVG	HR	RBI
918	.323	84	502

RUNNING THE NUMBERS

.365

Mauer's batting average in 2009, the all-time highest single-season average by a catcher.

3

Batting titles that Mauer has won, the most ever by a catcher.

5,372,606

All-Star votes for Mauer in 2010, the fourth-most of all time.

INSIDE INFORMATION

FAVORITE VIDEO GAME	FAVORITE ACTOR	FAVORITE TEAM	FAVORITE SPORT (OTHER THAN BASEBALL)
MLB The Show	Jim Carrey	Minnesota Vikings	Basketball

SECRETS TO HIS GAME

Throw Out a Base Runner Like Joe Mauer

Making the throw to second base can be tough for young catchers, since it's such a long distance. Even if your throw is coming up short, it's important to master the proper mechanics. If you do, when you improve your arm strength, you'll be able to get the ball to second base as quickly as possible.

[1]

Think about making a triangle with your feet, says Terry Steinbach, a former All-Star catcher who works with Twins backstops during spring training. When you're crouching down, your two feet should form the base of the triangle.

[2]

When you come out of your crouch, the first step (for righthanded throwers) should be forward with your right foot, making the third point in the triangle. Then step toward second base with your left foot and make an over-the-top throw. "I see a lot of young catchers running forward and leaning," says Steinbach. "But you want good balance when you throw."

[3]

Good throwing mechanics have to become a habit, says Steinbach. "A lot of times players get lazy and start dropping down, throwing sidearm or three quarters," he says. "But it should always be step and throw, over-the-top. I hear [Twins manager Ron Gardenhire] say it a million times during spring training: 'Step and throw, step and throw.' And he's talking to major leaguers!"

[+] When Mauer was a kid, his dad built a special device out of PVC pipe that he now calls the Quickswing. The ball would drop out of the pipe quickly, so Mauer had to act fast with a short, compact swing. That's a big reason he can now wait on a pitch until the last moment and drive it anywhere on the field.

[+] Mauer has had some problems hitting for power the past few seasons. He's had nagging injuries, and the Twins' new ballpark, Target Field, is one of the toughest hitter's parks in baseball. But the potential is still there.

"When he's healthy, he's a 25-home run, 100-RBI guy,"

[+] says an AL scout. "In recent years, there were balls that normally he would crush that instead he fouled off. But he shouldn't get anything less than 20 home runs and 80 RBIs [in a season]."

Mauer is also a top defensive catcher. Despite being big for his position (6'5"), he's quick getting out of his crouch to track down bunts or throw out base runners. In 2007, he showed off the arm that made him a

[+] star quarterback, throwing out 53.3 percent of base stealers. "He's unbelievably accurate [as a thrower]," says the scout. "He would just catch it, get rid of it, and it was right there on target."

KNOW THE DRILL

Many young catchers have a bad habit of coming out of their crouch before they move to block a pitch in the dirt. To practice blocking, have a coach or teammate stand behind you and ask the pitcher to throw pitches intentionally in the dirt. As the pitch is coming in, the coach should gently push the catcher in the lower back, down and toward the pitch. When practicing, use a tennis ball rather than a hardball. "Blocking a baseball with your wrist or forearm can hurt," says Steinbach, "but you have to learn not to be afraid of the ball."

IN HIS WORDS

"Although catching might beat you up a little bit physically and mentally, I love the demands that are put on me and the responsibilities that I have."

PRO FILE: JOSH HAMILTON

JOSH HAMILTON

BACKGROUND REPORT

>> Josh Hamilton always seemed destined for greatness. He wasn't just another top prospect out of Athens Drive High School in Raleigh, North Carolina. He was a once-in-a-generation talent, with a dazzling left arm (as a pitcher in high school he consistently hit 96 miles per hour on the radar gun) and a vicious home-run swing (his bat speed was once clocked at an otherworldly 110 miles per hour). Hamilton was drafted Number 1 out of high school in the 1999 amateur draft by the Tampa Bay Devil Rays, which awarded him a then-record $3.96 million signing bonus.

"I remember seeing him taking batting practice with the Devil Rays in 2000 during spring training, and I was like, 'Who's that?'" says former major league first baseman Sean Casey. "He was 18 years old and hitting balls farther than anyone else. I went up and introduced myself, and I said, 'That's one of the greatest swings I've ever seen.' I don't think I've ever done that my whole career."

>>Fighting Back

But things didn't go as planned for the sweet-swinging Hamilton. The clean-cut, churchgoing boy who kissed his grandmother Mary before every one of his high school games got mixed up with the wrong crowd in the spring of 2001, after he suffered a back injury in a car accident and suddenly found himself with a lot of free time away from the baseball field. After struggling with drugs and alcohol, Hamilton was suspended from baseball in 2004 and didn't return until the Cincinnati Reds snagged him from the Rays in the Rule 5 draft in 2006. When he made his long-awaited major league debut on Opening Day 2007, he received a 22-second standing ovation as he stepped up to the plate for the first time in Cincinnati. He landed with the Rangers a year later, after being traded to Texas for pitcher Edinson Volquez. "Texas had faith in me," says Hamilton. "I couldn't have asked to have landed in a better situation, with teammates that embraced me with open arms."

SMASH HIT
Hamilton was named the 2010 American League MVP after leading the league in batting (.359) and slugging (.633).

With the Rangers, Hamilton finally began truly fulfilling his promise. In 2008, he was voted by fans to his first All-Star Game and put on a dazzling show in the Home Run Derby at Yankee Stadium, hitting three home runs that soared farther than 500 feet. In 2010, he won the American League batting title and the Most Valuable Player award. "He's really all everyone said he was," says Boston Red Sox pitcher Jon Lester. "He's strong, he's fast, he can hit, he can run. He's got real strong hands. It looks like he doesn't swing at a ball. He just flicks his wrist at it and the ball goes forever."

>>Shining in the Lone Star State

Hamilton is a big reason why the Rangers, historically among baseball's worst franchises, has become one of the giants of the

major leagues. During the 2010 American League Championship Series, he hit four home runs (even though Hamilton was intentionally walked five times in six games) and led Texas to its first-ever World Series appearance. In 2011, the Rangers won the AL West and returned to the Fall Classic for the second consecutive year, thanks to another All-Star season from the player who has battled back from as much adversity as any player in the majors. "Sometimes I step back and look at how far I've come, and even I can't believe it," says Hamilton. "It's been an incredible journey."

BASEBALL RÉSUMÉ

HIGH SCHOOL
Athens Drive

MINOR LEAGUE TEAMS
Princeton, Hudson Valley, Charleston, Orlando, Bakersfield, Louisville (1999–2007)

MAJOR LEAGUE TEAMS
Cincinnati Reds (2007), Texas Rangers (2008–present)

CAREER STATS

GP	AVG	HR	RBI
589	.308	118	425

RUNNING THE NUMBERS

490
Distance, in feet, of a home run Hamilton hit on June 27, 2010, at Rangers Ballpark in Arlington off the Phillies' Roy Oswalt. The home run, which landed in the seats in right centerfield, was the longest ever hit at the ballpark.

130
Runs batted in by Hamilton in 2008, his first full season in the majors. Hamilton's total was the highest in the American League that season.

28
Home runs Hamilton hit in the first round of the 2008 All-Star Home Run Derby at Yankee Stadium, the most ever in a single round of the derby. During one stretch Hamilton hit homers on 13 consecutive swings.

INSIDE INFORMATION

ATHLETE ADMIRED AS A KID	SHOE SIZE	FAVORITE CEREAL	NICKNAME
Tony Gwynn	19	Fruity Pebbles	Hambone

SECRETS TO HIS GAME

Take Pride in Playing Defense Like Josh Hamilton

Hamilton is one of today's biggest stars because he doesn't focus only on putting up big offensive numbers. "I realize that if I go 0 for 4 there are still other ways I can help us win," he says. "I can influence the outcome with my bat, but also my glove. I can't make an impact every night at the plate, but I can in the field." Hamilton isn't lightning quick, but he covers as much ground as any outfielder in the game. "He reacts to the ball off the bat as well as anyone," says Rangers manager Ron Washington. "He has great instincts." During batting practice, Hamilton stands in the outfield and works on reading balls off the bat and making throws into the infield. "I practice a lot in the outfield, with the other outfielders, as much as I do in the batting cages," says Hamilton. "It's fun for me. During a game, I'd rather throw a guy out than hit a home run."

IN HIS WORDS

"Playing all out and aggressive and leaving everything on the field is the only way I know how to play. If my career gets shortened by injuries from playing hard, or I didn't get 10 years in because I played [too] hard, then that's the way it's going to be."

INSIDE HIS SWING

Hamilton used to take a step forward with his front foot when he swung at a ball, but he had trouble connecting with off-speed pitches on the outside part of the plate. So he started using a toe-tap technique. When he begins to swing, he brings his front foot back a few inches, taps the tip of the shoe on the ground, and then puts the front foot back to its original position. "It helps me stay balanced and stay back on off-speed pitches and breaking balls," he says, "and allows me to get to pitches on the outside of the plate and put good wood on the ball."

PLAYER ANALYSIS

[+] Hamilton is one of the most complete baseball players in the majors. He is most known for his legendary home-run power — "He puts on shows during batting practice; it's hard not to just sit back and watch the bombs he hits," says Rangers second baseman Ian Kinsler — but he also has one of the best defensive gloves in the outfield. Ask Texas general manager Jon Daniels for a memorable Josh Hamilton moment from recent years, and he names three defensive plays, all of which preserved wins for the Rangers.

[+] Says Phillies outfielder Raul Ibañez, "[Hamilton] plays the shallowest [outfield] I've ever seen, and he can still go and get the ball like nobody's business."

"Watching him play is exciting," says former A's pitcher Greg Smith. "The ball just sounds different coming off his bat, almost like a gunshot. You watch him track down a ball, you watch him throw a guy out at third base. Then he hits a ball down the line and gets a triple and it's like, 'The guy can run too? You've gotta be kidding me.'"

PRO

VEF

TEAM: **DETROIT TIGERS**

POSITION: **PITCHER**

HT: **6' 5"** WT: **225 LBS.**

BIRTH DATE: **FEBRUARY 20, 1983**

HOMETOWN: **GOOCHLAND, VIRGINIA**

LE: JUSTIN LANDER

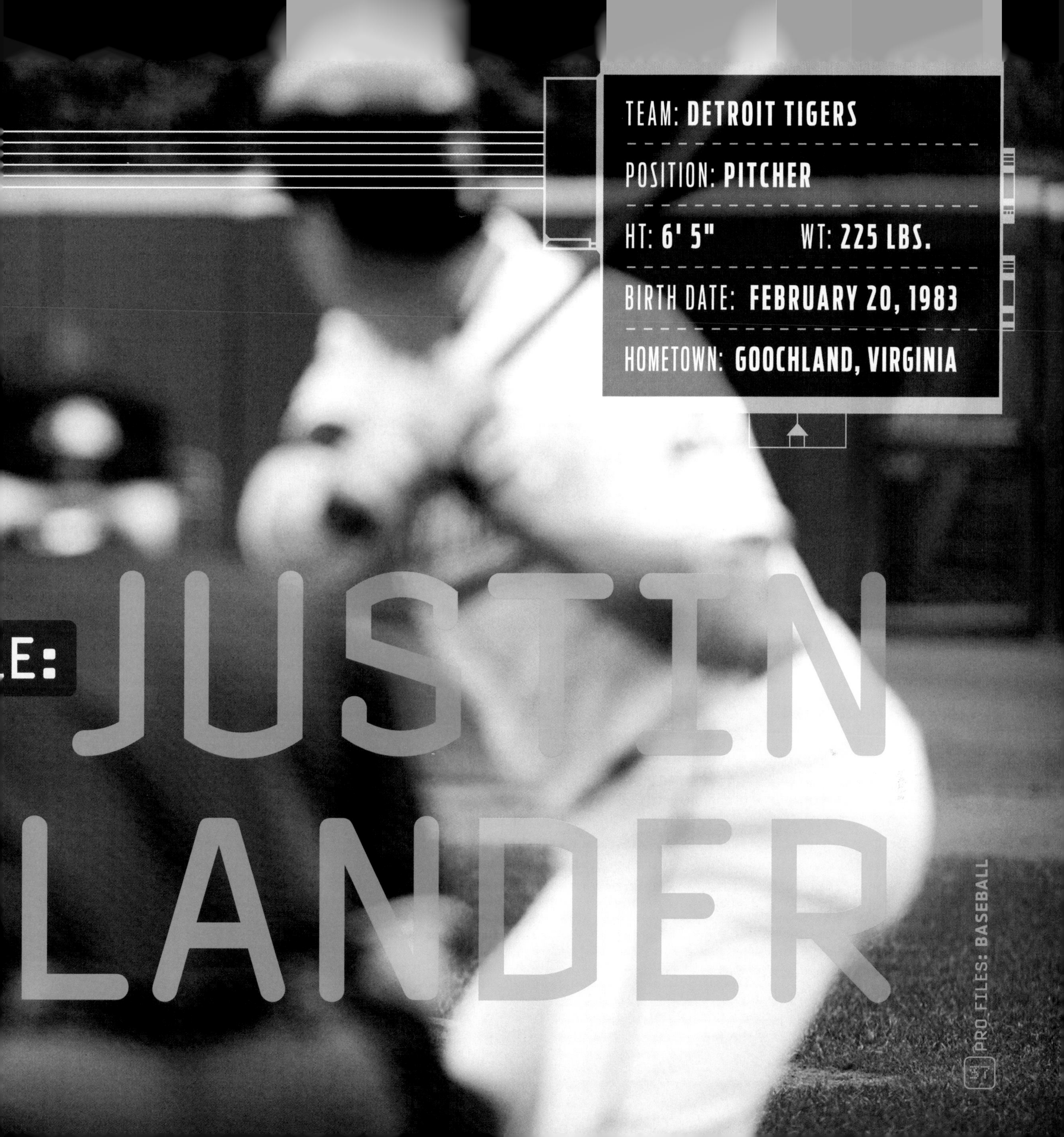

BACKGROUND REPORT

>> When Justin Verlander was 10 years old, he and his father were skipping stones across a small pond near their home in Goochland County, Virginia. His father, Richard, picked a rock and threw it as far as he could, his toss plopping halfway across the pond. Then Justin grabbed his own rock and chucked it across the entire pond. "At that moment, I was like, 'This kid has got a special arm,'" Richard remembers.

Verlander, the 6'5" ace of the Detroit Tigers, has always had a natural ability to throw hard and far, but he has worked at his craft, too. To practice long toss, Verlander would drag his family to a local football field, where his mother, father, and brother would relay his 100-yard throws back to him. When Verlander was in high school, his father hired a former college pitching coach, Bob Smith, to teach his son. From Smith, Verlander learned how to pitch to hitters, not just throw to the plate. "There should be purpose and knowledge behind every pitch that I throw," Verlander says. "The wrong pitch with conviction is better than the right pitch without it."

>>Rapid Rise

Verlander came into his own while attending college at Old Dominion, and the Tigers made him the Number 2 overall pick of the 2004 draft. Verlander's career began so smoothly that making further adjustments didn't immediately seem necessary. He was named 2006 Rookie of the Year, helping the Tigers win the American League pennant before losing to the St. Louis Cardinals in the World Series. In 2007 he threw his first of two career no-hitters and made the first of four All-Star teams. But he suffered a setback in 2008, losing 17 games, the most in the majors, while managing only a 4.84 ERA. Verlander quickly realized the importance of staying sharp and not growing complacent.

"For two years this game came pretty easy to me at the big-league

CAN'T BEAT THE HEAT Verlander won the 2011 American League Cy Young Award after leading the league in wins, ERA, and strikeouts.

level," Verlander says. "I'd just go out there, throw, and things fell into place for me. I'm not saying it is an easy game. I quickly found out that it's not. It just seemed that this was the way it was going to be forever. I guess, maybe, through that process I lost a little bit of my edge."

>>A Season to Remember

Early in the 2009 season, Verlander committed himself to being mentally strong by cutting out all distractions before he pitches and keeping his focus sharp during games. This approach led to his historic 2011 season: Verlander was unanimously named the AL Cy Young Award winner after completing the pitching Triple Crown by leading the league in wins (24), ERA (2.40), and strikeouts (250). A few days later, he was named the AL MVP, becoming the first pitcher to win the award since Dennis Eckersley of the Oakland A's in 1992 and the first starter since the Boston Red Sox's Roger Clemens in 1986.

Verlander's fastball is so fast and his curveball breaks so much that he struck out an average of one batter per inning while walking the fewest batters of his career (only two for every nine innings he pitched). His intelligence, his cannon arm, and his durability (he's thrown five straight seasons of 200 or more innings) are the reasons why Verlander is one of baseball's elite pitchers.

INSIDE INFORMATION

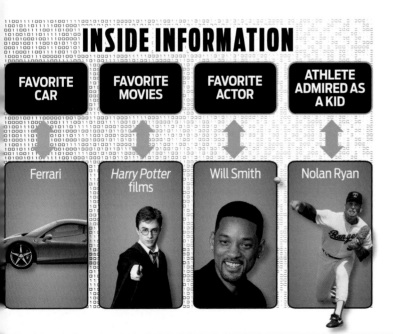

FAVORITE CAR	FAVORITE MOVIES	FAVORITE ACTOR	ATHLETE ADMIRED AS A KID
Ferrari	Harry Potter films	Will Smith	Nolan Ryan

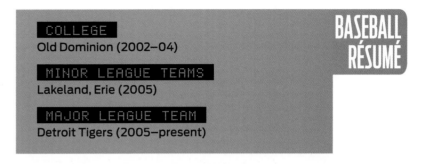

BASEBALL RÉSUMÉ

COLLEGE
Old Dominion (2002–04)

MINOR LEAGUE TEAMS
Lakeland, Erie (2005)

MAJOR LEAGUE TEAM
Detroit Tigers (2005–present)

CAREER STATS

GP	W	SO	ERA
199	107	1,215	3.54

RUNNING THE NUMBERS

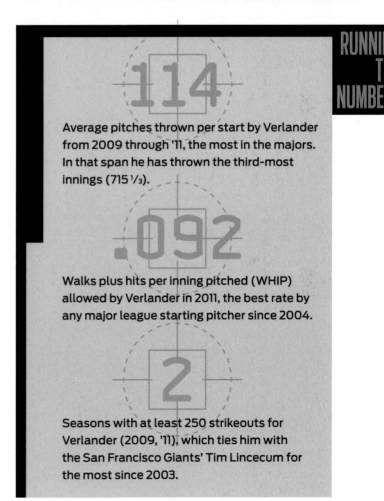

114
Average pitches thrown per start by Verlander from 2009 through '11, the most in the majors. In that span he has thrown the third-most innings (715 1/3).

.092
Walks plus hits per inning pitched (WHIP) allowed by Verlander in 2011, the best rate by any major league starting pitcher since 2004.

2
Seasons with at least 250 strikeouts for Verlander (2009, '11), which ties him with the San Francisco Giants' Tim Lincecum for the most since 2003.

SECRETS TO HIS GAME

Command Your Pitches Like Justin Verlander

Even the best pitchers struggle with control, and Verlander was forced to learn how to harness his pitches at an early age. As a teen, he was already a hard thrower — his AAU catcher, Mike Vranian, wore quarter-inch padded gloves under his mitt to avoid bruising — but Verlander wasn't the most accurate pitcher. Says Vranian, "The first batter would either walk, because Justin was so wild, or he'd strike out, out of fear."

Eventually Verlander's AAU coach Bob Smith implemented a rule that Verlander had to throw two simulated innings in the bullpen before taking the mound, in order to get him to settle down. Smith finally harnessed the erratic arm by forcing him into situations with little margin for error. A 15-year-old Verlander was made the closer for an elite 18-and-under fall showcase. "When a kid's backed in a corner, sometimes they react in a positive way," Smith says.

For his first save opportunity, Verlander entered in the bottom of the ninth with a 1–0 lead. His first 12 pitches — all fastballs — missed the strike zone, and he loaded the bases on three walks. Smith called time and jogged to the mound. "What are you doing?" he barked at Verlander, who responded, "I don't know." Smith chewed him out, saying he should never give "I don't know" as an answer. The coach then instructed him to throw only curves — and Verlander struck out the next three guys on 11 breaking balls, missing the strike zone only twice. Said Smith, "It was a defining moment for him."

> "It's hard for me to put a finger on what I know, but it's there. Time. Experience of pitching at this level for a while now. You log it all away, and it opens up a new game to you."

THE REPEATABLE DELIVERY

Verlander has never had to make major changes to his delivery, but over the years he's made tweaks. He's now mastered what's called a repeatable delivery. That means he's comfortable enough with his delivery that he can repeat it over and over again without having to think about it. His mechanics are simple and fluid, with his whole body working in sync with his arm. That repeatable delivery has led to better control. It also means less stress on his arm. Through six seasons, Verlander had never spent a day on the disabled list. And while most pitchers wear down as the game goes on, Verlander's velocity is still there late in games. During a no-hitter in Toronto in 2011, he threw a 100 mile-per-hour fastball to the last batter of the game.

PLAYER ANALYSIS

[+] Verlander has a powerful
[+] right arm, capable of
[+] throwing fastballs in excess
[+] of 100 miles per hour. But he's
[+] most effective when he's
[+] painting the corners, which
[+] makes his pitches extra
[+] difficult to hit. "He throws
[+] strikes," Rangers manager
[+] Ron Washington says. "He
[+] goes out of the strike zone by
[+] design. So when he's in the
[+] strike zone and he gives you a
[+] pitch to hit — this is easy to

[+] say, but it's not easy to do —
[+] don't miss it. Try not to
[+] chase."
[+]   A common strategy for
[+] hitters facing great pitchers is
[+] to be patient at the plate. The
[+] idea is that the more a pitcher
[+] throws, the more tired he gets
[+] and the easier it will be to get
[+] a hit. But that doesn't work
[+] against Verlander, who has
[+] averaged the most pitches per
[+] start of all major leaguers in
[+] each of the last three seasons.

[+] "You don't have to worry
[+] about building up his pitch
[+] count, because the pitch
[+] count with this guy just goes
[+] out the door," says
[+] Washington.
[+]   Verlander has been known
[+] to hit 100 miles per hour or
[+] faster even when his pitch
[+] count is at 100 pitches or
[+] higher. "With Verlander, you
[+] feel lucky any time you get a
[+] hit," says longtime big leaguer
[+] Orlando Cabrera.

PRO FILE:

JOEY VOTTO

TEAM: **CINCINNATI REDS**

POSITION: **FIRST BASEMAN**

HT: **6' 3"**   WT: **200 LBS.**

BIRTH DATE: **SEPTEMBER 10, 1983**

HOMETOWN: **TORONTO, ONTARIO, CANADA**

BACKGROUND REPORT

>> Joey Votto grew up in the suburbs of Toronto, Ontario, Canada — a country mad about hockey — but as a kid he preferred a different sport. In 1991, his parents gave him a baseball bat for his 8th birthday, a year before his hometown Blue Jays won the first of back-to-back World Series championships, and Votto was hooked. "I was a very big baseball fan," Votto says.

For nine or ten months of the year, Votto and his father would play catch every day after school, which was no small feat in Canada's cold climate. But Votto loved the time with his father so much that he would insist on going outside — even on holidays. "Remember this," his father told him after one outing, "because we just played catch on Christmas Day."

When his father wasn't available, Votto would walk behind the restaurant his parents owned and throw balls at a square target he had painted on the concrete wall. At the time Votto concentrated mostly on pitching, but he suffered an elbow injury when he was about 13. "I thought it was the end of the world," he says. It turned out to be a blessing in disguise. "I probably wouldn't have been a professional ballplayer if I didn't hurt my arm," Votto says. His real skill, he learned, was hitting.

>>Hitting the Mark

By high school Votto had found a group of friends who loved baseball as much as he did, so they would go hit every afternoon. "We'd hang out, and it was like our hobby," Votto says. "I don't remember watching TV or having time to play video games, but I do remember always doing baseball stuff."

That constant repetition and adherence to a practice regimen paid off. After Votto starred in high school at Richview Collegiate Institute, the Cincinnati Reds made him a second-round pick in the 2002 draft.

In September of 2007, Votto reached the big leagues and homered in the first at-bat of the first game he started. In May of the following year he hit three homers in one game against the Chicago Cubs, and he finished second in NL Rookie of the Year voting that season behind Chicago catcher Geovany Soto.

FIELDER'S CHOICE
Votto, the 2010 National League MVP, won his first Gold Glove in 2011.

>>Red Hot

Votto kept steadily improving until his game exploded in 2010. He led the National League in on-base percentage (.424) and slugging percentage (.600) while ranking in the league's top four for batting average (.324), home runs (37), RBIs (113), runs (106), and walks (91). He received 31 of 32 first-place votes to run away with the NL MVP award.

Pitchers were more careful with him in 2011. But Votto's discipline at the plate helped him lead the league with 110 walks and a .416 on-base percentage, and he still batted .309 with 29 home runs and an NL-leading 40 doubles. And, after steady off-season work to improve his fielding, he won his first Gold Glove.

Votto, still only 28 years old, is now established as one of the game's elite hitters for both power and average. His next goal is to lead the emerging Reds deep into the postseason.

HIGH SCHOOL
Richview Collegiate Institute

MINOR LEAGUE TEAMS
GCL Reds, Billings, Dayton, Potomac, Sarasota, Chattanooga, Louisville (2002–07)

MAJOR LEAGUE TEAM
Cincinnati Reds (2007–present)

CAREER STATS

GP	AVG	HR	RBI
617	.313	119	401

RUNNING THE NUMBERS

.418

On-base percentage for Votto from 2009 through '11, the best among all National League players over that time span.

31

First-place votes, out of 32, that Votto received in 2010 to win the NL MVP award. He became the first Reds player to be named MVP since Barry Larkin in 1995.

77

Years since someone had hit 10 doubles in five games before Votto accomplished the feat in September of 2009. The last player to do so was Pirates Hall of Fame outfielder Paul Waner in 1932.

INSIDE INFORMATION

FAVORITE VIDEO GAME	FAVORITE ACTOR	FAVORITE FOOD	FAVORITE SUBJECT IN SCHOOL
↕	↕	↕	↕
FIFA 11	Tom Hanks	Pizza	English

SECRETS TO HIS GAME

Hit to All Fields Like Joey Votto

Votto hit his first major-league-distance home run during batting practice at the age of 18. The lefthanded hitter smashed the ball down the rightfield line — "totally pulled," he says — and then it hit and bounced over the top of the wall. "It was like choirs started singing," he recalls. "It was such a huge moment for me. It sounds ridiculous, but little things like that mattered." The homer showed Votto his progress as a hitter. He got so serious about becoming a major leaguer that he used a wood bat in high school games. Now, the older and stronger Votto (6'3", 220 pounds) has power to all fields and he isn't focusing all his strength on yanking the ball for homers. "I can shoot a ball through the gaps now," he says. Even though he is an MVP, Votto still makes regular adjustments in his approach as he continues to establish himself. "[In 2010] I felt like every single at-bat, I had to go get it myself," Votto says. "I think you have to establish that at the beginning of your career. You have to prove [yourself] to the pitchers by being aggressive, getting a lot of extra-base hits, and doing some damage in tough spots."

GLOVE STORY

Votto admits that he used to struggle with his fielding as a young minor leaguer. "I was such a fish out of water when it came to defense when I was younger," Votto says. "I didn't know what I was doing there. I had to slow the game down." He accomplished that with lots of practice. Votto designed his own fielding drills, which he practices over and over with the help of the Reds' Double A hitting coach, Ryan Jackson, who lives near Votto in the off-season. "He's very organized," Jackson says. "You don't get where he is without being somewhat of a perfectionist. It's almost that he takes more pride in his defense." Says Votto, "Now the game is very slow, especially when I'm on defense."

PLAYER ANALYSIS

[+]   A lefthanded batter, Votto
[+]   knows how to hit, plain and
[+]   simple. He can hit for average
[+]   and for power; he can drive
[+]   the ball to leftfield and pull it
[+]   to rightfield. Over his last
[+]   three seasons he's batted .318
[+]   and averaged 30 home runs
[+]   and 100 RBIs.

[+]   But Votto is productive even
[+]   when he doesn't swing. In 2011
[+]   he led the National League by
[+]   taking 110 walks and had the
[+]   NL's highest on-base
[+]   percentage (.416) for the
[+]   second straight season. After
[+]   his MVP season in 2010, pitchers
[+]   were a "little more cautious" in
[+]   throwing to him, he says.
[+]   A big reason why Votto is so
[+]   disciplined at the plate is that
[+]   he is a "very studied player of
[+]   this game," according to Reds
[+]   rightfielder Jay Bruce. Votto
[+]   watches a lot of
[+]   video of opposing
[+]   pitchers and
[+]   constantly
[+]   practices in the
[+]   batting cage.
[+]   And though
[+]   Votto admits he
[+]   wasn't
[+]   comfortable
[+]   playing first base
[+]   early in his career, he has
[+]   worked to turn that weakness
[+]   into a strength. In 2011 he won
[+]   his first Gold Glove. "Joey
[+]   saves us," Reds manager
[+]   Dusty Baker says. "All he
[+]   needs to do is stay healthy
[+]   and don't change anything."

IN HIS WORDS

"I felt like a lot of people blazed a trail for me. At some point I just started saying to myself, 'Why don't you set your own standards? Why don't you see how good you can be?'"

PHOTO CREDITS

Cover John Biever (Pujols); Tom Dahlin (Verlander); Robert Rogers/MLB Photos/Getty Images (Verlander headshot); Brad Mangin (Hamilton)

Back Cover Robert Beck (Halladay); Chuck Solomon (Longoria); Al Tielemans (Votto)

Title Page Bob Rosato

Table of Contents
Mike Ehrmann/Getty Images (Pujols); Robert Rogers/MLB Photos/Getty Images (Longoria); Nick Laham/Getty Images (Halladay); J. Meric/Getty Images (Mauer); Ron Vesely/MLB Photos/Getty Images (Hamilton); Robert Rogers/MLB Photos/Getty Images (Verlander); Rob Tringali/Getty Images (Votto)

Albert Pujols (pages 6–11)
Al Tielemans (2); John Biever (3); Darren Carroll (6); Focus On Sport/Getty Images (Marichal); Courtesy of Movieposter.com (*Gladiator*)

Evan Longoria (pages 12–17)
Greg Nelson; Damian Strohmeyer; David E. Klutho; Movieposter.com (*The Sandlot*); Getty Images (steak); Bob Rosato (2); Erick W. Rasco (batting); Porter Binks (quote)

Roy Halladay (pages 18–23)
Chuck Solomon; Al Tielemans; David E. Klutho; Nino Mascardi/Getty Images (steak); Getty Images (model plane); John W. McDonough (2); Robert Beck; Illustrations by Colin Hayes

WELCOME HOME
Slugger Albert Pujols scores during Game 7 of the 2011 World Series, helping the St. Louis Cardinals win their 11th championship.

Joe Mauer (pages 24–29)
CJ LaFrance/ZUMApress.com (opener); Brad Mangin (2); Valerie Macon/AFP/Getty Images (Carrey); Courtesy of IGN (*MLB 11*); Bob Rosato (2); Al Tielemans; Kyndell Harkness/Minneapolis Star Tribune/MCT/Landov (blocking); Illustrations by Colin Hayes

Josh Hamilton (pages 30–35)
Bob Rosato; John Biever; Denis Poroy/AP Photo (Gwynn); Mike McGinnis/Cal Sport Media (cleat); Damian Strohmeyer; Greg Nelson (2); Al Tielemans

Justin Verlander (pages 36–41)
Fred Vuich (opener); Greg Nelson; Warner Bros./Everett Collection (Harry Potter); C Flanigan/FilmMagic (Smith); Chuck Solomon; John Biever; Mark Cunningham/MLB Photo/Getty Images (portrait); Bob Rosato (7)

Joey Votto (pages 42–47)
Al Tielemans (4); Courtesy of IGN (*FIFA 11*); Pascal Le Segretain/Getty Images (Hanks); Getty Images (pizza); Getty Images/Tetra images RF (books); Chuck Solomon; John Biever

Credits Page David E. Klutho